Anna's Song

ARTHUR OBERG

Anna's Song

University of Washington Press

Seattle and London

Library of Congress Cataloging in Publication Data
Oberg, Arthur, 1938–
  Anna's song.

  I. Title.
PS3565.B4A83   811'.5'4   79–4847
ISBN 0-295-95681-X

Publisher's Note

The poems in *Anna's Song* were selected and arranged by Arthur Oberg's friends and colleagues Richard Blessing and the late Joan Malory Webber after the poet's death in February 1977. The publisher wishes to express appreciation to them and to Barbara Oberg, the author's wife, for their contribution toward the preparation of the final manuscript, and to Professor Blessing and Mrs. Oberg for their help in seeing the book through publication.

Acknowledgments

These poems have appeared in the following publications: "A Dream of Coastal Houses" and "Two Studies for a Bloodmoon" in *Carleton Miscellany;* "A High, New House," "A Dark War," "Grandfather," "Composition for Wind and Hand," "Occasions for Flowering," "The Smell of Burning," and "The Wounds of the Small Beasts" in *Shenandoah;* "Sorting Out the Signs" in *Southern Review;* "Islington Suite" in *Painted Brige Quarterly;* "Elegy for Cathy" and "After the Royal Palms Were Brought Down" in *Poetry Northwest;* "The Hillhouse" in *Quarry;* "Giving Her Away" and "The Seven Lovely Sins" in *Western Humanities Review;* "Going Back" in *Jeopardy;* "Obstructed View of the Arbitrary and the Profane," "On the Random Brightness of Letters and Numbers," "Voting in Favor of Happy Endings," "Fable for the Sad and the Beautiful," "Tempering the End of Summer's Fall," and "Finding a Language for Beatrice" in *Poetry;* "Talking with Raphael" in *Stand;* "Deaths of Fathers" and "Learning American Grace" in *Ohio Review;* "Agape" in *World Order;* "Loving" in *Burning Deck;* "Centering" in *Northwest Review;* "Wedding Song" in *Rocky Mountain Review;* "Poem for a Quick Wife" in *Salmagundi;* "Begin, Again" in *Yale Review;* "Walking" in *Quarterly Review of Literature;* and "Anna's Song" in *Iowa Review.*

Contents

TALKING WITH RAPHAEL

VOTING IN FAVOR OF HAPPY ENDINGS

ANNA'S SONG

COASTAL HOUSES

Divining a Propitious Site for Building

You advise me to bring my compass for
wind and water. To obtain the best site.
I am Emperor all over, without his robe,
orange carp, or birds. You never question
ways the needle will work and point outside
China, devise a home, shine like some famous
Japanese garden stone, brought to its resting
place—wrapped in silk, in time to music

A Dream of Coastal Houses

This is our ground—the armoire
we encouraged up the wood stairs,

the dippy paper we matched, flower
to flower, leaf to wall and stem,

the Yoshi-iku woman reflecting
you, through silk and glass. Her

feeling, stylized hands lift,
out of herself, yourself, *yours,*

comforting me. If house with
walls, I imagine the First Universe

of grass, of grasscloth made. Bride
and groom. Flesh as grass. And

the House's fourth wall, down.

Walking

You stand in a pink robe
with gold braid.

The early, January camellias
flame on their dark

green leaves, extend, open
their coastal sway.

You take up, take in black,
wet loam, the sunny

floor, the wasp moving
his farthest

corner of wing, on a leaf.
So far, and so

far. Beyond, I mark the
Quick, bright place

Where your robe   , falls

Seasons Are Passing from Our Lives

1. The mouth of summer

Begin with what will last,
just enough light to see
the whitebird hold—rise and

ride—take the air as seabird

Back on the lake: to know
how dawn comes on, but
always that there is wood

for the small fires we keep,
for tables we break bread
on, sure as bass, fireflies,

knives sharpened so thin
hear them in low sleep,
long after dream is gone, light

big as trees and fine as moths
come out in the night to look around

2. The mouth of winter

Here, we are groundsong,
the swell under the hill
tells it will not be long

before the dead give over
land they can never plow
whatever the implements

land that curves as far
as the sea they would keep
that will never be ours

except as we hear it now
coming over the hill—
under us, still, groundsong

A High, New House

1.

Flowers, that puzzle your face.
What informs this day—

accusations of long weariness,
wondering over my preference

for lashing out at you, where
Arboretum walks come together,

divide, parallel the long lake.

2.

Blue, your eyes are green
in that other light. If

we are ever to move beyond
anger, we will again be

seated among old cups and
plates, agreeing to keep

the blue ridge along
a white edge, within

eye's range, each piece in
place, finer with years of

wilful, and gentle use.

3.

Today, we come home, late.
In the house, there are more

flowers, more light than
the rooms ever, once,

could contain. Returning to
them, with this look on them,

we admit dark paneling
we never liked, finding

a place for the bonsai
we accept to keep inside

a few days at a time
so that it might live,

lovelier for that, for
the waiting it holds us

to, toward the days ahead,
it can again reside with us.

4.

Darkly, we go over
the first, lonely time

the rains ran from the
top of the mud hills,

down the streets to
the house where we stood

looking north, the band
of ship canal water, beyond,

mountains you said we had
to take on trust, forgo

seeing them, for days, know
them explicit as flesh,

as the woman I was learning
more than to dream

into this house
when the rains came,

when there could
be no question of

rain or rooms or wife.

Walking It Off in Seattle

We were running over the old grounds.
No one could have had such cool
hands in such warm air. New
moon, I saw you hold your
both hands so long, so far
down in the cold, running troutwater.

Nothing too slight
for night, or day.
Naming may not keep them,
there. Still, I say them—
collanders, the first crop of berries,
herbs on the sill, in the March sun.

Days of fog, and I am learning how
to keep such lonely counsel, the
air-routes the city lost to other
cities, whatever access we want
or need across the Pole; in you,
I learn impunity never walked the planet,
and punishment has nothing to do with love.

Getting through Sundays

Night comes on. I write one
of nine letters I owe. My wife
rolls an orange across the wood
floor, without a word. Monday,
I will walk out at eight, with an
umbrella in mind, against the rain.

Sorting Out the Signs

It is March, and not one
camellia has chosen
to open for us. In the old

Seraband, the shower of arrows
is harder to figure out, the
blue wools, rotten at the nub.

And the rain is rain we can hear
coming down, not the rain we
have come to expect—from March

to March—a rain always falling,
and so never falling, so far
North, upon this coast, a quirky

corner, mimicking love. And,
today, this rain, falling into
tonight, falls back to bodies,

the peculiar things they are,
in the face of rain

The Wounds of the Small Beasts

1.

No gods in these mountains.
Rainier, a deceptive strawberry
cone; at Snoqualmie, fifteen below.
Snow telling us loss is

always loss, the fur animal
must always bleed and die
for the world, weeping where
words click short, and sweet love.

2.

The child altar boy bearing
help the priest needs
To say Mass, and be done.
The glass popes in the Vatican

turning the wine to gall,
the bread to dust, ash in
the mouth, deriding baroque
And medieval vanities. Death

is always death. And John
sees a different man,
in scorn of flesh and
blood, pick up the keys he had.

3.

On the clearest days, ice
plays false, and trails
are no help to what
is allowed. To the North,

Mt. Baker affronts our sight,
sends us into woods
To bring back the beast,
bleeding and sad, wearing our

face and the pain that is
always pain, denial that loss,
taken up, can ever dull
when there has been so much

love, and of such kind.

A Dark War

From the market, we carry
the parsley home in clumps,

shaken out of the pot. Home,
I repot the close roots, spreading

them gently out, place the pot
on a white plate. In a day, the

leaves already turn to the sun's
source, to whatever light we own.

2.

Upstairs, two studies sprawl
with books and prints. A black,

leather couch roots its steel legs
to the floor. Making love on a cheap

rug may be all we have. I point
to the new wisteria shoots

that climb into the highest reach
of a house, barer than Wyeth beams

that stand, awkwardly out, to our eyes.

3.

Tomorrow, the March begins its crawl
downtown, past windows where

jade once lay. They will snatch
stones worth anything out, cover

displays with cloth, tugging us back
to kitchens with milk, and plants that rise.

4.

Love, we have never been here before.
But we will be here, again. Before

one more day makes its slow way back,
I will set the traps for rats

whose sure pellets I find. I am
angry and sad. Once, I boasted

a voice that would never crack. It
cracks, used by, less and less used

to, a dark war that is in the walls
of a house, windows we fought to keep,

angles and wood and lines, before we
signed on the line: CONDEMNED FOR HUMAN USE.

Making Things Available

You are never done with ferrying to
the islands, determining the right
proportion of sun and shade for extravagant
fern, watching the planes drop near the cone
of the strawberry mountain. You crack open
the core of shiny promises, the fine
ritual tone to say home is where the
jar goes empty. What is it the tide
makes us swear of the pair walking water?
Let him wear this bone ring on his little
finger. Let her carry her best slotted
wood spoon to whatever new house they may go.

Imari

My image of that other coast, morning
lost, not my sense that it was different

from these rocks, this sea, this air.
Downstairs, you are singing. I am too

superstitious to call it happy, or sad.
The phone makes only outgoing calls.

The cat knows how soft he can purr,
and still sound large. This sea,

a country wide from that other coast,
tells of The Three Friends of Winter

(plum, bamboo, pine), washes in under
the window, moves in pleasing the eye

blue, white, under the same stairs and sky.

Elegy for Cathy

Not oranges or stones, words refuse to bob
until we bow to them, take them up. Simplicities
of the kitchen hum for us. You brew java in
cups, grind the strongest beans, butter the
best holiday bread, share it against the time
we will have to talk, and of her death. Last
night, before taking off your dress, you cried
for *all that blonde hair in a wood box.* The
island ferry was again late, and I was out
looking for other ways of scoring a song for
death, wasteful because by water and so young.

The Hillhouse

December first, and I fear the
house that became too precious,
its cups and bonsai, balancing
under an artful bloodmoon. Carp

that swam outside, the golden
carp grown sacred to the king.
December first, and I make
other choices, do and remember

other things, when we cooed
of the soft perversions, kept
in a drawer; when we argued
the matter-of-factness of saints,

how they must manage more than
brandy and music; the total
lay of cards, across the board,
a game of musing, weaving blood

as it fell, into the cloth—
as quickly as it fell—
forgetting what winter would
demand, even before it came,

hinting another moon, the
thin, dark cups, the laps
unused to balancing, the one
card you knew she held from

you; blood, more red than cloth.

Building an Ark in Seattle

We started joking about an ark.
It rained every day in November.
Half way out of December, we have
the same odds. We distinguish rains
depressing and purging, indistinguishably
fine, those that do havoc with felt
hats. Now there is nothing but fog,
and fog. Freeway speeds posted at 50
give us the laughs. Before the high alpine
tree is tagged, the Christmas deer
bagged and cleaned of shot, we welcome
bids for building the ark. Over Remy Martin,
by tonight, we will give the builders' names out.
In good time, we will hang the best name on the ark.

DEATHS OF FATHERS

Saying It the Way It Is

Confessional, we were never
even knee-deep in history
or moss. Looking out on the

Commons, I rethink what
details I would write if
told to be *pushier,* to tell

all: that there is short
singed grass as far as
the canal; that my wife

bought me a traveling
corkscrew for our anniversary
of glass; that my child

attends a birthday
of a friend who celebrates
because he's 7½, who asks

his guests what each of them
makes of it: 7½; peep-show
favors which expose the Trojan

horse; strawberries with
double cream; a slide built
with him in mind: no fated

day or sad night in the bed
in this house, no having to
deny some fireman's son his

own crescent of fire in which to stand

Legacy of an American Child

What fell to you: the uncut
wood for winter, snow, the name
KEEPER OF THE FLOWERS. You
sulked in the barn, cried
over kings & dwarfs you failed
to keep happy. You had no door-
frame in the event of a twister,
no dog to howl the yard. If this
was America, it lay months from
summer, miles from the coast,
lights, or any town. You had knife,
towel, water. You said you never
had a father. You bend down, part
the straw. Lonely only child, on
your knees, making up the barn.

Grandfather

I move toward your rude, brown
oratory in snow,

below the Austrian peaks you loved.
Dead, you received a wood stand

for Masses to be sung, the one
concession made, (buried in

Protestant dress). What remains—
the glass of wine you

took with each meal, your eye
for young girls in the

house, the way an apple came
to your hand,

peeled in one piece. When you died,
they remembered only where your

Protestant wife lay, parceling out
the other pieces in the house

where you crossed yourself
before a table they always

Knew would fall to themselves.

Giving Her Away

Fifth wheel. The only thing that makes sense
is that it not make any sense at all. He
sleeps through debates about engraved or
printed invitations, what is a small wedding
or a large wedding. He asks the impolite,
obvious question—bed together, but why
marry? She talks to him, and in her voice
is petal-fall, and that credit will come easier
to them. The young man stares at him and
at the wall. Fifth wheel. If he goes away, maybe
it will go away, they will go away, he can send her
away again to read books, travel, meet a man and marry.

Going Back

Low, a thousand miles from you,
we ease a new painting into place.
White walls. Light from the fire

lights your sunny sea house,
vintage wine-years put down.
Glasses, talk in a room, empty

but for a few chairs, a fur
pillow cut from an old coat
by hand. We thought you happy,

gentle with each other. Fingering
your separate addresses, we
remember you stooping together in

the bright hall of hanging plants,
to let us in.

The Consolation

At the dinner table's head,
he hugged his wife
for some consolation
we could only guess,
for the other women he had
had, for the need, still,
to have her as his wife;
before, I had never even seen
him kiss her, once. On the
white card at my place,
I wondered for each of our names,
relieved that no one would
say grace, yet have grace on
his mind, remembering that small
gesture, earlier in the night—
a man, before the table, before
a lovely wife, holding her to him
like a first bride, consoling her
for things he called our lives.

East, East of the High Grasses

Light drags the soldier, scraping
through the wars. In the marshes, deep into
the year of the horse, the generals command
what they can command, cursing the pamphlets,
the thin chickens, rags (they drift down whitely
across the countryside) striking the backs of
cows, drift down like fear into the hands
and hearts of peasants who know
that to bend, or not to bend,
is death.
                In the West, to the death
we dance. The rain, carrying the public chants,
the single poem read against that war,
aflutter with gut hate and love, the rain
sorrows for all she bears,
and for what bears her down with the sorrow of children.

Divorcing

You try to build a
letter around it,
a telling context.

Small craft fails.
Simpler, to drift
apart. You invent

reasons, moments or
years later, to com-
fort your friends.

You need no comfort,
hearing the sea wash
in, under your window;

you insist he stand
under the biggest tree
in the sweeping meadow

as you count the
seconds between claps
of thundery lightning

moments of surrender
you had no truck with
before the storm

before it became
your tale, blowing
out to sea, going

out by a different
door you enter, just
to find him, gone or

writing your own poems
over, finding the right
poem for the line you

always had left over
when he called you come
to bed and try to sleep

Deaths of Fathers

IN MEMORY OF MY FATHER, 1910–71

1.

Going older,
how to trust
finding some

way around
the softer
places.

Maudlin, caws the old bird.

2.

One man grows quiet in the last week.
Another goes off into the woods to die.
Each forgets, on purpose, to tell his
son, or nonexistent son, or wife.

3.

The yellow freesia manage
their spiky blooms in the easiest
way—coming to flower, puckering,
imperceptively, letting go their
yellowdust into the small
of the large room.

4.

They tell me it is Elijah's mantle
I must take up. But the reedy feel
of cloth hurts me too much. If I
take up anything, it is a face,
the flinty bits of wit that fell,
the compassion the man had
for what he touched.

5.

Slow skies.

Beyond hurt—
fatherless words.

Under my sign,
Arthur, once prince,

I wait to pull
the sword from stone.

Mystery, bone,
your eyes on me.

6.

After words, seeking some gentler rhyme—the
prose-bone of death still rises and sticks
in my throat. I cannot undream space, time,
the long spaces between words, the places and
occasions doubtful of love. *Love is witty
in his cups, and sane,* I once tried. But,
tonight, in London, fingering your death,
I look out of the highest window. Chimney
pots surely, slowly march across the sky.
Now, broken and in disuse, they are as orange
as ever, and still too close to me. They
are silent, could never speak. They offer
nothing. *Let go. Make peace with them.* If
they find voices for anything, it is the speaking
of my own dreaming, my own words. The prose-

bone. Death. After the fact. Going more deeply
down, I uncover another voice, the only voice,
my voice, perhaps. *What is, you are.* If the
broken chimney pots again could smoke and flame,
I would go out to them, hear of common,
insistent things like deaths of fathers, my own
father, once and only and always sons.

TALKING WITH RAPHAEL

Agape

I am the stone-cutter finding
the right stone,

sorting the colors, sifting
texture and weight.

The plum-colored cornelian
piece meets my eye.

It will do, to perfection,
I decide. All night,

I manifest my love for the
bright stone, carving

clusters of loving fruit,
choosing to carve on

both sides of what will be your stone.

Talking with Raphael

FOR MIKE & ERIC

Whatever it must have
been like: to talk with

him of brushes & media, wingy
things & half-light. Or,

with the other, the earlier
one: to talk of God, His

high plans for men, somber
as noon when the trees

are too heavy to stir, to
give off more than the heat

of full sun in a high sky.

Two Raphaels, or
more accurately,
four of them—

two versions;
& behind them,

the angel, &
the angelic man.

Four Raphaels, all
of them, wrong.

If I had to engage either,
image him, imagine them, here,

we would talk of buttons,
spoons, stones picked up

along the coast, the particular
green of lemon leaves, &

I would know what you meant
when you said of him—
it was like talking with Raphael.

Centering

you cannot center
the pot, unless
you know your own

center,

have the arrow
fly to the mark
unless you let

it go wide,
first, and far,

separate the
words of a friend

wheat/chaff

tell the shoes
you lost yourself

from the shoes
the gypsies stole

from you last night
while you dreamed

through

whatever dark kept
you from centering
the morning star

A Day in the Country

I hold up my hand, stake
out the marshland around Rye,
point from the leaded window

upstairs in the sea-looking house
to cows that look stupid,
stupidly small, their brown

and white spots coming at
intervals too regular to
be real or even possible;

just say there were cows,
blotches of them, eating
grass to the ground:

a dream of slow cows
let loose in a marsh town

Simple Light

I throw out my voice
in search of better berries, the
best fish and game around for miles.

I send Freud, Jung to different
corners of stubby meadow to
see morning breaking: sun, moon at

large in the same sky. When
I fall, hurtling past lodgepole
pine, it will be upon water.

Composition for Wind & Hand

Wet socks, wide wind. Another birthday.
Song, the needling hassle whether art

will out, or in. For something more or
less at stake than things at hand, beyond

the reaches of fidelity, Beethoven moved
30 times in 50 years, sometimes without

the time (I catch myself) to unpack, put
back piano legs, composing only by grace,

grace notes, his keyboard open & in front of him.

Strategies in Extremis

1.

I couldn't wait until you told it all
or got the dents out from the wobbly cup,
or found a right-sized table for the cloth.
Long poets dwindle, dawdle into wrecks.
One rises in his dressing gown in Kent,
as good a getup as any in the house,
stub stick against the slowly warming dawn.

2.

So many others ran to die by their own hand,
as if the gas or ice would fix them, hold
a place for them in some eternal company.
"See how sick & tired I told you all that time I
was; no window opened where you said, *see land.* "

3.

There is another method, music, Muse.
It comes. She waits. I match five
fingers to my other hand, read late.
Leaves *shimmer,* the airy ones that move
outside my window. I bring them *in, here.*
I pronounce them good, the ways they hang on.
You believe them what I say they are.

Arthur Schimmelpeninck Is Dead

It is easier to do your own dying, harder
to imagine someone else's death—Lucky
Wagner, Esther Feinkind, Arthur Schimmelpeninck.
When they told me Schimmelpeninck *passed
over*, I thought of tornado and cloud in the
same breath, wished I were musician or painter:
the three notes that would signal his entry,
the lonely color for cock crow, the single
line for face, rubbed out for the hundredth
time, and still not right. When hands are
shaking, I want to know the reasons. When
letters come, I want to know which to answer,
and the ones to lay down on the odds time
improves the grain or taste. Schimmelpeninck,
I see your women, their hands at sides aching to
hold you back from a grave more like a well,
a sure shaft into the earth. The flowers they
carry arrow the depth of descent, where your
head and feet lie down. What do you know?
Nothing of all this I would guess, or of one
bird vying for full sway over the North snow sky.

Learning American Grace

FOR THEODORE ROETHKE

I vowed never to write a poem for you.
I veer East Coast, even walking your rounds.

But we meet. Beyond anecdotes friends
of yours keep, beyond the one time I heard

you read in New York, your shirt-tails, out.

You rode out the long & longer lines.
You were hearing strange things at the end.

When you died, I thought you least
& most yourself.

Long years of rain, & I still wonder you down—
about whether the dead can also help.

Why the tears in your head?
Down your face?

Phallus, throbbing
like an exposed frog's

heart, after, open to clinical
silver? Ending alone.

Every silence in place.

American grace—getting through Sundays,
a slow coastal rain.

It is there you can help.
Your foot, kicking a stone.

Your head, cowled,
& the voice,

sharing the lowest joke on the seawall.

VOTING IN FAVOR
OF HAPPY ENDINGS

The Transfer of Absolute Power

Treading water in so much splendor
when all you aimed at was walking,
walking without going under, or
was it all a lie—treading water,
gradually moving into the light one
morning, the queen of the night sorry
to see her reign over, and you pulling
the moon, taking the sky, saying we
shall have a hand in the run of tides

The Seven Lovely Sins

1. Covetousness

the fox's drool
looked small, close

up to it. In my
garden & under my

grapes, he would be
a different fox.

2. Sloth

so, slowly, you
dealt with him,

because you feared
he would wake

to wake you from
the same dream

you both slept.

3. Lust

flesh, bone, that
metaphor without

brakes, divorcing
even when it is

not romantic, all
out for the next

honeypot, enough
snatch for the

night, not enough
for the next &

the next night
after that night.

4. Pride

in your painting,
the wine plume

at the sea's
edge, even when

there is no
horse to ride.

5. Envy

the smallness
of it all,

taking it back
to when it was

she first took
to wearing lapis

lazuli, blue
against white,

and you wore pearl.

6. Gluttony

the round
face that

lost the
lines

that were
a mouth.

7. Anger

that dark
flashing light

burning in
burning on

dark sun
that will

not go out

even when
it is time
for sundown.

Obstructed View of the Arbitrary and the Profane

The field is out of love with the sky,
unloving, letting the wheat go its way,
over land heavy with the same birds

coming to end in a road, a fence to keep
horses from cows, men from women they
say they love. As for the gods, when

will we let them alone, or let them return
us a face from clay, better still a face
from the mountain, stone and below snowline.

Wedding Song

You learn what is the stars, the sea,
light before you can say morning.
Time goes funny in your hands. You
watch the banana tree keep its leaves.
After, yellow fruit has to be let
down. Each lashed leaf cries to the
hillside almond, olive, and pine,
trees that go on into the next century.
In the town square, two steps behind
the mongoloid child, the father walks.
He dreams the child away from him, goes
alone upon the promenade of palms,
the *balcon* under his feet, the sure
sea, beyond, beating out something—
a dirty tune on black, sharp rock—
for a wrong child made under no moon
she called to him that night hold just
so high, *o moon so right for love.*

For This We Came to Spain:

to trace the aqueduct arch
in air, with one finger,
feed the fire with beachwood
dry enough for burning, learn

February's fictions, wait
for the Janus-face to tell
of short views and long views,
having it both ways, and one

way looking full into the sun

.

Lowering Nets at Dark

FOR JIM AND SUZANNE

You write from your OAKHAUS in Columbus. Love
goes out to you from one of our interminable
seahouses facing east. The details of your
second worst dinner still make us laugh. What
about *the first?* Tell us of that black feast.
Here it is autumn in Andalusia; in some towns,
leaves veer red and even desert their trees.
Late into last night, Barbara cracked walnuts
on our tile floors for apple pies. Amandita
makes me puff up my cheeks so she can hear
the air pop. The garbagemen sing dirty Spanish
ballads at four in the morning. I grow tired of
living the one-line, stand-up Jewish comedian.
I debate the virtues of making resolutions
for New Year's, or giving up something for
Lent. I promised you a happy letter. Remember?
As I run this back, only fear and sadness look or
leak out. You know enough sadness, sad letters.
But you asked us to write, whatever the news.
Now you have all that we were hoarding. Imagine
measuring weather by lowering nets at dark.

On the Random Brightness
of Letters and Numbers

Why can't lightning always
take down the tree? If we
insist on less, what a poor
forest that would make. As
for the news that will come
from the provinces (strapped
to the side of some beast un-
mindful of mud or dusty shoes),
promise us this time the news
will be good, sweet, down to the
last word the eye dreamt it could
read. Obstinate print: given the
choice of going over into law, or
remaining wood that could make a
bed—any old design of stars—for
two, love. To welcome the night in.

Extended Sonnet for Two Men

Call it Lagos, Spanish or Portugese, and by
the sea. One man makes copper pots, cannot
write his name in letters. He's never been
to the next village. He knows fruit to eat,
fish worth cleaning because they're sweet.
In his sleep, he hears gossip and prophesy.
*These are iron times, so deal in silver and
gold.* On his dream walls, red bison give
way to the dawning of numbers—fives, tens
acknowledge foot and hand as ways of
counting stores, counting love. Black carbon
traces the fish within the bigger fish
done by a man who lived three hundred miles
inland. He's never been outside his cave
or heard of Lagos. He's never seen the sea.

After the Royal Palms
Were Brought Down

The fishing boats shift their nets,
pick up and head for better grounds.
You ache to be wise, ache because

the dark tells you nothing is what
all is about; even the child knows
the stone planter of frogs goes

empty one night, for the whole year.
There are more idiots upon the town
than it can hide. *Don't mention*

it, the bank teller cries, the large
notes counted out twice. His green
eyes, white walls of this house,

the intricate, dark roses you cut
at dark, all say *nada, nada* is:

some of the morning boats come in,
fish float in, swim against the tide

Voting in Favor of Happy Endings

The birds are too insistent for
quieting. They go from olive
bough to olive bough. Even if
we could catch them, they wouldn't
keep the fire going for very long.
The horizon blurs just where you
usually see boats making it, with
small motors, to shore. Threaten
to bring in a string of professional
mourners, how will that alter the
day? Even vials of third-rate
tears are too expensive to price,
impossible to weep. Last night,
boring took on a third dimension—
high, deep as sky, almost as wide.
This morning, I went out to count
how many new almond blossoms had
fallen during the night. It was
disappointing. I had heard no wind,
expected to hear, find (this time down)
only the occasional petal on the ground.

Occasions for Flowering

In the lesser sites, the digging peters out.
Go there, your boot uncovers shards and Roman
coins as sudden as you walk, as soon as heel
puts down. You have only to bend and dream
the slow clock back. Along the coast, wild
flowers gone to straw wait to be snapped
or else their blues and yellows go to brown—
unpicked, unloved; the pitcher that might
have held them, empty on the sill. Clay
is the color and the substance of the cliffs
that edge the sea, that long poem of which
all poems are part. If art shows our dying
anything, it is that perfect poems can only
be lived out, imperfectly, borne out with time
in time. Jasmine, outside, returns to things
as sure as air. Its flowers, yellow, white,
know enough to save themselves for certain
hours. They spend themselves the way grace
falls, how Andalusian light appears
in the courtyard, mornings, without one worry
about ever having to conquer anything at all.

ANNA'S SONG

Anna's Song

She made me promise to write a real story this time,
without the holes that could be held up to the light or the
dark. She told me in her special way. In the way she patted
dry the slices of eggplant after salting them to draw out the
bitter tastes. In the way she let me make love to her. In
the way we settled on a piece of Wedgwood or Imari. It
was an arraignment, and an agreement. I called it Anna's
song.

How many thank-you notes Anna wrote after the wedding,
I never knew. What I remember were the last three we did
together in our heads. One was for a pair of cocktail glasses
that might have been for some later anniversary of glass—
"how perfect," she (or, really, the two of us) wrote, "they
are to the fit of the hand." The second had to manage a
green, porcelain plate with red berries—"how it matched a
luncheon cloth we loved." And the third—a carefully
hedged thank you for something to this day we can't name,
and from a distant relative we never heard from again. For
our own daughters, we would recommend, if marriages are
still sung in twenty years' time, against sending calling cards
to say they are at home.

We stood on different sides of the hedge or wall. When I wrote her a poem, I placed her sometimes on my own side to talk with her more easily as a woman and a wife. And then I put her on the other side to have her say things that really were more on my own mind. The house we lived in had views of the Olympics and the Cascades. We sat in chairs in the same room, made love in the bed we joked of as being always in the same place, beneath shutters I put together by hand, slat by single slat. Making love from different rooms was hard enough to handle in the movies. In our own life, I preferred our familiar bed. And I knew that Anna preferred it to other arrangements our friends talked about and, sometimes, confronted us with. *Their* rooms. *Their* bed. *Their* house. I staked out our own corner of land and called it, in a tiny poem, "Anecdote of the North." What mattered was that it was ours.

It was the telling that counted. And whether the analyst was smarter or dumber than the priest. Choices, again. And if choice was some terrible exclusion, I preferred it to living in the muzzy-fuzzy way of keeping everything semiattractively open, or closed. In fact, I chose against analyst *and* priest. It was the one possibility I could make out of Anna's song. If I misinterpreted, I lived with the danger and spent more time listening.

My daughter, five and an important half, stands in the tub, playfully running the washrag between her legs. Laughing at me with round, also brown eyes, the me, looking at my older daughter. When the children are in bed, Anna and I share the love seat. Its one spring is going; the other, gone. Its dyed purple fabric turning an unpleasant blue. We talk about the house, or the different house, three or four houses distant in time, from this house, when we will be alone. Now, we are more than a man and a woman in a house. We talk about what it means to be a man and a woman housed with two lovely daughters, with no sons who will have to go to the wars.

"Well, are you glad you got your son?" They were the first words my mother greeted my father with, when I was born. I have heard the story, since I was able to hear and see and talk full sentences, a hundred times a year. Face to face, by letter, and, breathily, over the long-distance phone. To this day, it is lightyears away from the kind of thing Anna would ever think to say to me.

I have had so much wine that I have trouble finding the bed. One can't get drunk on a shared bottle of vintage red, had with a five-course dinner cooked by a wife. But on this bottle I have, or am. Once, a bottle; now, a tale to be put down for the years. Anna tells me I am silly. She reminds me of the birthday card on which I called her Squirrel. I agreed to call her Kanga; she, to call me Roo. But Squirrel? Totally inappropriate. I can't remember, even if my life depended on it. Anna swears it so. She is wrong about small things, but this strikes me not as small. I must be wrong. Anna helps me to bed and is still smiling in a way that touches me without offending me. Also, you must have guessed with me by now, part of Anna's song.

Farmhouse with Red Marsh

Your body knew the dark
spots of the sun, and
why the bed was proud
and never had to knock
on wood, that it was
never cheap to say how
two of us could enter.

Poem for a Quick Wife

You are the historian in the house.
In dream and by day, you are always

tugging me back to something I have
missed—a date, some face I would

have left unturned. It was you found
Ruskin's stone for us. I pointed

the wild violets close about the base.

Another Sunday of rain. And the
rain is bent on getting in. *Let*

it in, you say. You will have nothing
to do with Puritan Sundays in our house.

Seven years, and I am still learning
something about having you about as wife,

the kind of historian you insist on being for me.

The Costs

We have different centers,
ways of falling, & coming

apart. Yet the matter is
not detail, or one of direction,

the sharing, or not sharing
of feeding chocolate
to a great-grandmamma in bed.

I think of the poem
for which I was grateful,

the rejected voyage to
the moon, the knowing

that one & one shall,
& shall not, always

be two; so, if the lions
owe the Christians nothing,

I can still dream the large,
airy & airless arena, back.

The splayed woman would hide
in the ink drawing he made

amid millions of lines &
ghostly faces, but I will

not let him have her, or hide
her, so. Her ambiguity lies

in the realism she makes,
he makes of what we own.

The bright shards that will
neither cut, nor bleed,

I once began, for a wife,
to wonder why I denied her,

& before morning; this morning,
even, because of slow fog,

it is the lyric house

I build, & that builds,
to light, & full of light,

exact, right, always ours
under the sign of a marriage

I spend with you to know
the sure arc, to where you are,

an older tune, from another life,
déjà-vu, at dark, with you

the mistress of the only inn
I ever saw you, serving in, &

talking at, the only inn, once,
you simply colored in for me, in air.

The Poet to His Wife

The blue glass
that holds the
ivy in place,
spills its light

in the slightest
sun, darkens the
ivory netsuke by
the year: a miller,

his sack of grain
full at his glad
feet; his hand,
over a water gourd.

The netsuke warms
in my hand, smooth
but warmer than
glass. I fill in

the smile that has
worn. My wife
sleeps on in our
bed. The miller's

contentment stays
on my tongue like
a stone. I envy
him the way I fear

my wife sees me go
to the setting down
in this early light
to this advantage she

does not have—sadness
turned round, long
enough to be given
back as love, poem.

Knowing the Best Hours

Burned batter, the spatula
ruined, me stomping off
upstairs, trying to assign
someone the bloody blame;

you tell me you are taking
the children out; I hear
the distance of the words,
the time in that tale

the man held up a frying
pan to hit his wife
because he was angry
because he was sad

because his daughter
kept thinking she was
the one to blame, blame
they sat down to & ate

while the mother took
the children out, looked
at the sea, pulled out
the weed from the spoke

that made the wheel stop
that made the father go
out on the beach, just
to fight with the sea,

so far out he could not
hear what she sang, back
on the shore, how wit is
born of work & grace,

how love is man & wife,
building a December house,
trapping hours, sun & light,
quickly gather the other in

The Smell of Burning

1. You

Are learning anger, &
anger. All night,

you keep staring me
down, throwing

me your knives. "I'm
gonna clean your

clock," you laugh.
Waiting that time,

I am growing the
glove I will

throw down for you.

2. Catching on

Like the pepper plant, you
learn to live in a warm house,
doing beautifully with new, green leaves.

Doing, learning so well, I wonder
was it wise to take you in?

3. He

Stops writing lyrics at thirty,
grows petulant, forgets the kisses
she likes, the single flower, raven hair.

Once, she unpinned him, held him.
Her kind of man.

4. The comfort of numbers

Will you bring the house
around you, burning the roof,

floors, the seamy walls?
Just to savor saying

it was "my first wife" said that?

5. The burning child

Playing it out on paper, paper.
Go in to her.

Go in to fetch her out.

Fable for the Sad and the Beautiful

Here where even the light is what I
bring to these pages. Anger, days:
the telling of what is human, and
therefore late. Dune grass blown
over the coast's face. A March moon
in April. Your love told to me by
keeping my name, in thinking of change
as how we moved to bed, what we made
of it, how we let madness go for some-
body else's hat and head. I walk
toward you, this is the poem I gave
to you as a black rose when I mistook
the poem for the rose, the dwarf for
the man in the tale who railed at love.

Keeping It Turning

Nudge me, & you
will see why I seem

hard, no concern
for you on my mind.

What is my heart
like, after the
metaphors of mathematics

split apart, less
brilliant than diamonds

shining & exacted in
early morning sunny air?

I nod to violence, heads
above the sentimental cry

for musk & musketry
had on the same bright night.

I open
& am not
the flower

I wanted to
show to the world.

You are open,
say the
meaning of *open*

fractures just
by our looking up,

that I am not what
I thought, or you dared
me be: open, open, or

for all that exchange,
flower at all.

She

listens to the squirrels eating into the eaves
to the sound of the ways we replace things
on the shelf, plate by honored cup and plate

waits to hear us say what has changed, what
is over for as long as her life is concerned
stops writing, counts on guilt for her paint

watches the pots on the sill turn, in every
way but toward the light the leaves will
need to climb and make her claims on us

she can withhold love forever, for so long
and the jade plant gives up more than its
usual, extravagant darkness of greenleaves

our own plant she has never seen or dreamed
love made in a house 3,000 coastal miles away
windows bellying out to catch light even dark days

Begin, Again

Maybe it takes years to speak
in the unwearied, scary voice
that "I" allows. Yet, once, out

with it, I am saying I am afraid
for you and for your words that
spell the sexual dark back to death,

the woman eternally bruised, lucid
and shrill about the men I thought
she loved. There must go other ways,

I say to you, now. I, to you. That,
and nothing else. Remember that
Paddington morning, shifting slowly,

Then rising from bed, or the even
rows of roses in Hamburg's gardens
lit by the candle, its cupped head,

I sent on its way—alone, gently,
but sure—down the darkening Seine?
We cannot always go away to come back.

Still, I have never felt so much need
and will to place these words for you
to say it is light, the light where we are.

Tempering the End of Summer's Fall

Maybe the sun or the sun's patterns
weren't accidental on the wall.
Or this morning's cold, making
the study once again unusable
for weeks at a time. Of course
winter can't and won't be forgotten.
Casual, deceptive. June and September,
gone with the curtains you packed
away with those birds that hung
on, in their own ways with boughs.
Only one man's left who knows
anything of leaded windows in
all London, and he's in France.
Windows and gardens. A cold walk.
Your joke about a necklace of scars,
how lost beads seem of greater price.
Toward recovery, I lean all my force
in small hope to get you back.

Finding a Language for Beatrice

That utter amazement
before a sheer world,
taking it apart to where

it all began. Some lean
on poems the way others
lean on mountains. How

can we come again to what
astonishes us, tenderness
in sex that is respect, and

never weakness, sure love
we lean toward because it
draws us toward the center,

woman and man, glad at the
source because it *is* source,
passing mad folk by, under

the light side of the moon

Islington Suite

1.

Sun starts me writing after weeks of rain.
Fronting this storied house, iron-grille work
comes clear enough to show its painted grapes,
and overpainted vines. I listen from the highest,
whitest window, wondering, if you hear me, feel
the same scars, between them, the exact,
familiar distances?

2.

It is too easy to be formal and abstract,
to trust to rhythms that shy away, fear
to break off. So laugh. Trust puns.
The dance again starts, pricks and princesses.

3.

Row houses. Gardens in the back.
Out back, the downstairs sculptor walks.
The garden's all a giant paper mushroom,
a garden party whim to be moved out, used
in a night. On Call. Rush Order. (Her
name is on his clipboard, in the dark.)

He is uneasy as I watch him paint
The final stripes and dots.

4.

Another day of sun. Last night
you told me I again would write, and
love, not in what order. The sculptor's
gone to raising newish props, to please
another woman's costly urgings. I dodge
him to have nothing, once, to say to him.

Upstairs, you turn the sheets
down, smooth for love, as wife.
After words.

It is not love is second best, but all.
Before, after words. Loving words.
And in that order.

A Garland for David Hartley

AND FOR BARBARA

From idea to idea
to the final
happiness of all

mankind, maybe
thereby, to God.
Hartley's wives,

two of them—
the one, gone
mad, the other,

dead from having,
trying to have
a child. In his

late years, for
the Stone, Hartley
took the waters, ate

200 pounds of soap (his
pound of wax for
the Virgin?) to cure

himself and prove
the world right.
He died at Bath.

The waters still
bubble up from some
underground source.

Hartley took the
Stone with him
when he died.

My wife sits
reading Hartley's
daughter, letters

to painters,
painter herself,
around her, a sure

brilliant circle
in Georgian Bath.

Daughters, wives.

The philosopher's
stone. Philosophy, hand-
maiden to the arts?

Wife, what does
one tree tell
us of the wood?

Happiness: the
way wood comes to
the hand, weighs,

and wants to fly;
to know you do not
have to be my wife

just because you are.

Loving

FOR BARBARA

I hazard mockery
or mistake. Letters,
held up to the light,
whichever way I hold
them, are postmarked

in the future. For
watermark, snake.
How is it your body
clears as I say
take this swordhilt

for joy, this ivy
for rooting in glass,
this child. It begins
TAKE, breaks off,
swims toward me, some

extravagant, dark
fish I let get away.

Inventory before Closing

You like me nicely troubled, owner
of my own tidelands, red tide in the
May of each year on the Sound. About
art, you are right as the fish that
fall to us, the clams inside the mark-
ing line: verse *is* trouble, nice or
unengaging, no sweet balance of fruit
got with small gold weights, antique brass.

Two Studies for a Bloodmoon

1. Dark

In the end, we are simple.

I poke the gut,
unstoke the fire.

I slow back to you,
untying the thread,
light, at the source-head.

2. I promise you

the lovely, deadly diminutives
little one, little one
tell me

I go back, trekking
through the impossible
garden

lifting you line by
line into air to say
I am never through